Who lives on my farm?
Can you name the animals?

Sky

words
Beverley Morel | illustrations
Christian Fisher

Well hello to you. My name is Sky.

I live in France on a farm with my donkey family,
my human family and lots of other animal
families.

I LOVE eating all the wonderful food that grows
here. What are your favourite things to eat?

yummy
yummy
in my
(empty)
tummy
yum
yum
yum

My Mum, Dad and Grandpa arrived here together from something called a Donkey Refuge. It's a place where donkeys can go if they have not been looked after properly.

They were brought to the farm, and I was born 3 months later. I was soooooooo small that I could be picked up and carried. Now I am 3 years old and big and strong.

yummy yummy
in my
tummy
grass and weeds

I live here with lots of animal friends.

I live with chickens, sheep, ducks, goats, cats, dogs, goldfish and lots of insects and animals that only come out when the humans are indoors, like mice and moles and foxes and all sorts of others that live in our woodland.

Can you name all my friends?

yummy
yummy
in my
tummy
hay and straw

My job is to help save the planet.
I know, how cool is that!!!!

Every day I have to eat the grass.

Every night I have to eat hay.

I also get given all sorts of other
delicious things to eat.

Of all the jobs a donkey could
have I have the best one EVER.

I LOVE my job.

yummy yummy
in my tummy

apples and
carrots

Everyone on the farm is really kind, except the
Magpie bird.

One day he whispered in my ear, "You're a
little donkey. How can one so small make a change
to the world?" and he laughed and laughed.

How I cried! Perhaps he was right. How could
a small donkey make a difference?

yummy yummy in my tummy
gorse and bramble

Grandpa came over and asked, "What's
wrong young Sky, why are you crying?
I have never seen you this upset before"

"Oh it's the Magpie bird.
He called me a little donkey too
small to make a change to the world."

yummy
yummy
in my
tummy

barley
straw

Grandpa sighed. "Oh Sky, you shouldn't listen to that Magpie bird. He's a trouble maker and is always up to mischief. Look around you" said Grandpa, rubbing his nose on the ground.

"Look at all your friends. They are working with you because that is what friends do. They help each other and, oh wait a minute......."

And I knew what was about to happen and even in my sad sad moment I started to smile.

yummy yummy in my tummy
pears and turnips

 Just then Grandpa did an enormous sneeze. It was sooooo big that it blew all over the land. Insects everywhere ran for cover. Some were picked up and blown over the grass, some hid in the flowers in the meadow and some burrowed further into the soil.

"Oh Grandpa you are so funny. No one makes me laugh like you do."

Can you name some insects?

yummy yummy
in my tummy
bamboo
shoots

And that made Grandpa smile too.

"How lucky we are to live with all these wonderful bugs. All helping to make sure the plants grow and make the soil rich and healthy. This is what happens when we all work together."

I sighed, "Okay but how does that help me to save the planet, Grandpa?"

yummy yummy
in my tummy
daisies and
thyme

So Grandpa explained.

"As you eat the grass it grows back so you become the lawnmower. When you eat the trees or bushes they grow back so you become the gardener. And you turn all of this into super poop."

SUPER POOP!!!!!!!! Can you imagine having super poop? It is just so so awesome.

yummy yummy
in my tummy
wild radish

Grandpa continued.

"Everyone loves your poop. Dung beetles roll it around and scatter it onto the soil.

"Then the worms come up and take it into the soil and others feed on it too. It is super food for the soil."

yummy yummy
in my tummy
sweetcorn
plants

"The more that lives in the soil, the healthier the plants and trees.

"And if everyone takes care of the soil, grows lots and lots of plants and trees, our planet will be a much healthier planet to live on and that, Sky, is why what you do helps us all.

"Pretty awesome for a little donkey of 3 years old." And as Grandpa said that he stood up tall, so proud of me. And there is nothing better than knowing Grandpa is proud of me.

yummy yummy

yummy

in my

tummy

turning

into

poop

And I sighed out loud. A loud contented sigh.

It is really beautiful where I live. So many beautiful flowers in the meadow,
so much for me to eat and surrounded by all my friends. All working
together.

I really do love my life and my job to help save the planet.
And if I can do it then perhaps you can too.

Beverley Morel owns and runs Ferme du Bourdicou where she is surrounded by donkeys, sheep, dogs, cats, chickens, goats, goldfish and more. The farm is run with a simple philosophy running through everything. It has to be respectful to nature AND it must be fun doing it.

@ferme_du_bourdicou

———————

Christian Fisher is a British-born illustrator currently living in the US, where he is surrounded by his family, a dog, some squirrels and the odd white-tailed deer.

thisfinchisrare.com